ALMIGHTY VOICE AND HIS WIFE

ALMIGHTY VOICE AND HIS WIFE

A PLAY BY
DANIEL DAVID MOSES

PLAYWRIGHTS CANADA PRESS
TORONTO · CANADA

PLAYWRIGHTS CANADA PRESS
202-269 Richmond St. W., Toronto, ON M5V 1X1
416.703.0013 • info@playwrightscanada.com • www.playwrightscanada.com

We acknowledge the financial support of the Canada Council for the Arts, the Ontario
Arts Council (OAC), the Ontario Media Development Corporation, and the Government
of Canada through the Canada Book Fund for our publishing activities.

 Canada Council   Conseil des arts
for the Arts   du Canada

 ONTARIO ARTS COUNCIL
CONSEIL DES ARTS DE L'ONTARIO
an Ontario government agency
un organisme du gouvernement de l'Ontario

 Canada

 Ontario
Ontario Media Development
Corporation

Cover and type design by Blake Sproule
Cover photo of Michael Greyeyes by Nadya Kwandibens, courtesy of Native Earth
Performing Arts

LIBRARY AND ARCHIVES CANADA CATALOGUING IN PUBLICATION
Moses, Daniel David, 1952-
Almighty Voice and his wife / Daniel David Moses. -- 2nd ed.

A play.
ISBN 978-0-88754-897-0

1. Almighty Voice, 1874-1897--Drama.
2. Cree Indians--Saskatchewan--Drama. I. Title.

PS8576.O747A64 2009   C812'.54 C2009-903524-3

Fourth printing: February 2017
Printed and bound in Canada by Imprimerie Gauvin, Gatineau

INTRODUCTION

It has been eighteen years since *Almighty Voice and His Wife* premiered at the Great Canadian Theatre Company in Ottawa; seventeen years since Native Earth Performing Arts produced it at the Native Canadian Centre in Toronto.

In 1991, a contemporary Native theatre was less than a decade old; a group of artists in Toronto had come together in 1982 to collectively create works like *Native Images In Transition* and *Tricksters Cabaret* for the stage, establishing Native Earth, while in Saskatchewan, Maria Campbell was making *Jessica* with Linda Griffiths and Paul Thompson. It would be 1986 before Native Earth produced its first scripted play, Tomson Highway's *The Rez Sisters*, and the rest is recorded history. Daniel David Moses was part of those early days, serving as playwright-in-residence at Native Earth, which resulted in the 1988 production of *Coyote City*, and the poet became the playwright.

Since its premiere in Ottawa and its second production at Native Earth, *Almighty Voice and His Wife* has been published several times, anthologized in *Staging Coyote's Dream*, and studied by students and academics the world over. However—how-ever—I truly believe that the times have finally caught up to Daniel's bitingly funny, achingly sad, wickedly astute, deceptively simple little play.

I am just not sure how many theatregoers were ready to receive the message in the early '90s. *Almighty Voice and His Wife* is all about the white gaze, about what an Indian looks like. White Girl, the wife of the title, has so internalized the white gaze that in the second act she becomes white, by means of whiteface.

Ah yes, the dramatically different second act. So many viewers, so many critics, so many readers, have been driven to distraction by the seemingly incongruent two acts. Yet the structure is one of the many brilliant touches in Daniel's brilliant play; how better to show the internalization of the white gaze than by performing it, complete with song, dance, spotlights, and stage makeup. Do you see us now?

Almost two decades after its premiere, Canadians have a whole lot of experience with which to receive the play: an ongoing discussion with First Nations about land claims, the Royal Commission on Aboriginal Peoples and its recommendations for a renewed relationship, the naming of Nunavut, *North of 60*, the Apology, Dudley George, James Bartleman, a growing concern about human impact on the environment. All this visibility, all this discussion, of Aboriginal issues and contemporary Aboriginal people, have created a different sensibility around First Nations and the representation of Aboriginal people in the media, the glass-eyed god. This is a canonical play, *Almighty Voice and His Wife*, whose time has come around again.

Yvette Nolan
May 2009

A NATION IS NOT DEFEATED
TILL THE HEARTS OF ITS WOMEN
ARE ON THE GROUND.

—*Cheyenne*

Almighty Voice and His Wife was first produced at the Great Canadian Theatre Company from September 20 to October 12, 1991 with the following cast:

ALMIGHTY VOICE   Billy Merasty
WHITE GIRL   Jani Lauzon

Directed by Lib Spry, assisted by Cat Cayuga.

The play was next produced by Native Earth Performing Arts at the Native Canadian Centre of Toronto from February 11 to March 8, 1992 with the following cast:

ALMIGHTY VOICE   Jonathon Fisher
WHITE GIRL   Pamela Matthews

Directed by Marrie Mumford with Larry Lewis.

CHARACTERS

ALMIGHTY VOICE   At first a young Cree man, early twenties, Kisse-Manitou-Wayou, also known as John Baptist, later his own playful GHOST.

WHITE GIRL   At first a young Cree woman, early teens, the daughter of Old Dust and the wife of Almighty Voice, later the INTERLOCUTOR.

The action of Act One incorporates historic events that happened between the end of October 1895 and May of 1897 on the Saskatchewan prairie, at and between the One Arrow and Fort a la Corne reserves. Act Two occurs on the auditorium stage of the abandoned industrial school at Duck Lake.

ACT ONE

A projected title: "Act One: Running with the Moon."

The projected title: "Scene One: Her Vision." A drum beats in night's blue darkness. The full moon sweeps down from the sky like a spotlight to show and surround WHITE GIRL, asleep in a fetal position on the ground. The drum begins a sneak-up beat, the moon pulses in a similar rhythm. WHITE GIRL wakes at the quake, gets to her feet, and takes a step. The drum hesitates. A gunshot and a slanting bolt of light stop her and block out the moon. Three more shots and slanting bolts of light come in quick succession, confining her in a spectral teepee. She peers out through its skin of light at ALMIGHTY VOICE, a silhouette against the moon. He collapses to the beats of the drum, echoes of the gunshots. WHITE GIRL falls to her knees as the teepee fades and the moon bleeds.

The projected title: "Scene Two: The Proposal." WHITE GIRL is by the fire, stripping meat for drying. ALMIGHTY VOICE loiters at a distance.

VOICE   Hiya. Hiya. Hey girl, I said, "Hiya."

GIRL   I heard you the first time. I'm working here.

VOICE   Oh ya?

GIRL   I am. And my dad doesn't like it, you talking to me.

VOICE   Old Dust? What's he got to worry about? He's winning over there. I'm just talking.

GIRL   It's not your talking he's worried about.

VOICE   What you talking about?

GIRL   You never mind.

VOICE	What you talking about, girl? Hey White Girl, what you talking about?
GIRL	My dad says you already got a wife.
VOICE	What's that got to do with anything?
GIRL	I hear you already had two others.
VOICE	You don't have to believe everything you hear. White Girl, you know something? I think you got pretty eyes.
GIRL	I got no time to be told my eyes are pretty.
VOICE	You're pretty fierce for a little girl.
GIRL	You should leave little girls alone, Almighty Voice.
VOICE	You're not that little, little girl.
GIRL	I'm working here.
VOICE	You're big enough.
GIRL	Go away.
VOICE	Is that the way they do it at that school? That's not the way my mother does it.
GIRL	Spotted Calf doesn't know everything.
VOICE	She knows how to strip meat. Here, let me—
GIRL	You could get cut.
VOICE	You're pretty fierce all right, little girl. You are like Spotted Calf.
GIRL	What?
VOICE	My mother's not as pretty as you.
GIRL	Go bother my brother for a while.
VOICE	But he's not as pretty as you.
GIRL	Sure he is. He's my brother. You know what?
VOICE	What is it, White Girl?
GIRL	My brother, Young Dust, he likes you.

VOICE	He's my friend.
GIRL	No, Almighty Voice, he likes you. He thinks you are the pretty one. Your wife won't kiss you? Well, my brother will.
VOICE	You're a crazy one.
GIRL	You're right. I am a crazy one. As long as you know. But my brother does want to kiss—
VOICE	I don't want to talk about your brother.
GIRL	Look, he's coming this way.
VOICE	What? No he's not.
GIRL	But Young Dust does like you.
VOICE	And I like you.
GIRL	I'm just a little girl, Almighty Voice.
VOICE	A little girl working away.
GIRL	You could get cut.
VOICE	I want to kiss you, White Girl.
GIRL	My father's looking at you. He sees you talking to me.
VOICE	Let him.
GIRL	You got to talk to him first, you know.
VOICE	I don't want to break that hand game up. All right, I'll go talk to him first.
GIRL	Then we'll talk.
VOICE	Just talk? What will we talk about?
GIRL	The wife you have now.
VOICE	What wife?
GIRL	The Rump's Daughter.
VOICE	Oh ya.
GIRL	You're going to send her home to her father.

VOICE	She won't go.
GIRL	She will go. I'm going to be your wife now. Your only wife. You can't feed us both. Well then, my father's waiting to talk to you. Go on.
VOICE	Crazy.

SCENE THREE

A projected title: "Scene Three: The Wedding Night." A second fire in night's blue. A gunshot and a slanting bolt of light. The reverberations become a social dance beat on a drum and bring up the rest of the teepee of light. WHITE GIRL enters it and sits. Then ALMIGHTY VOICE enters. The drum and teepee fade.

VOICE	Hiya, wife. I said, "Hiya, wife."
GIRL	What can I do for my husband?
VOICE	Come here. Look at me. Leave that be.
GIRL	Does my husband want some tea?
VOICE	Your husband wants his blanket.
GIRL	There. Your blanket's ready for you. It's snowing out. Shall I go for wood to build the fire up?
VOICE	Can't you be quiet, girl?
GIRL	Shall I tell your friends to be quiet? Shall I tell them to go away?
VOICE	They'll go when they're full.
GIRL	Do you want more to eat, husband? I'll go get some more.
VOICE	Stay here with me. Look at me, White Girl.
GIRL	That was a wonderful cow you brought for the feast. It was so fat.
VOICE	You didn't eat much.

GIRL   I'm stuffed full. I have never eaten so well before, husband. Now my father will have to admit his daughter is well-fed. You are such a hunter.

VOICE   It was only a stupid cow. What's wrong, White Girl?

GIRL   I was thinking about my mother. She would have made him come. And your father. How could the Mounties take him? The day before our wedding.

VOICE   They're stupid. Look at me, wife.

GIRL   I don't want to be a wife. I don't want to be a woman. That school—I don't know how. I'm only thirteen. I'm crazy.

VOICE   You're not crazy.

GIRL   I am. I am.

VOICE   Come here. Let me hold you.

GIRL   No, it's too dangerous.

VOICE   It's not dangerous. Hey, come on, pretend I'm your brother.

GIRL   No, you're my husband. I don't want you to die.

VOICE   You're not going to kill me. You're going to kiss me.

GIRL   I have bad medicine in me. I went to that school. The treaty agent took me.

VOICE   But you got away, girl.

GIRL   School's a strange place. All made out of stone. The wind tries to get in, and can't, and cries. It's so hot and dry, your throat gets sore. You cough a lot, too. I used to even cough blood. And they won't let you talk. They try to make you talk like they do. It's like stones in your mouth.

VOICE   You're here now.

GIRL   I liked it there.

VOICE   How could you like that?

GIRL   They said I could live there forever.

VOICE   What are you talking about?

GIRL	They said everybody at home had died of the smallpox. They said I could live forever but I had to marry their god.
VOICE	Hey, you're my wife now and I'm alive. Everybody's alive.
GIRL	He's going to kill you. He's a jealous god.
VOICE	He's another one of their lies.
GIRL	They say he's everywhere. He can see everything.
VOICE	He's got nothing better to do than watch us?
GIRL	They say he's like a ghost.
VOICE	Hey little girl, even your dad didn't know for sure about us and he watched you like a hawk.
GIRL	Or a white bird. They say he's like a white bird.
VOICE	A white bird? A white bird in here?
GIRL	He made the smallpox.
VOICE	Let's get that bird out of here! Where is it?
GIRL	You crazy, he'll kill you.
VOICE	Hey, little girl, I found it! *(He mocks flatulence.)*
GIRL	Stop that. You're crazy.
VOICE	Oh ya? Both of us? Made for each other. *(He kisses and caresses her.)* Little girl, my White Girl.
GIRL	Wait, husband, wait. I'm afraid.
VOICE	Don't be. I'm brave now I got you for my wife.
GIRL	But I'm afraid.
VOICE	What is it now, girl?
GIRL	It's the bad medicine. They gave me another name when I married their god.
VOICE	Shut up about their god! I don't want to hear it!
GIRL	They called me Marrie. It's the name of their god's mother.

VOICE	What's wrong with White Girl? White Girl's a good name. They're so stupid. That agent has to call me John Baptist so I can get my treaty money.
GIRL	John Baptist. That's the name of one of their ghosts.
VOICE	I'm no ghost. I'm Almighty Voice. Why can't they say Almighty Voice?
GIRL	I'll call you John Baptist too.
VOICE	You're not the agent! You're my wife.
GIRL	It's so he'll kill the ghost instead of you, husband. That god won't know it's us if we use their names.
VOICE	So I have to call my wife Marrie?
GIRL	Yes. Their god won't be able to touch us. Just call me Marrie.
VOICE	My crazy White Girl.
GIRL	Call me Marrie, husband.
VOICE	Marrie. Marrie, will you kiss me now?
GIRL	Yes, husband.

They kiss, caress, and begin to undress.

VOICE	Crazy Marrie.
GIRL	John Baptist.
VOICE	My little girl.

SCENE FOUR

The projected title: "Scene Four: Flight." A drum beats in darkness. WHITE GIRL pretends to sleep by the second fire. ALMIGHTY VOICE enters at a run, drops to his knees. The drum fades.

VOICE	White Girl, wake up.
GIRL	Go away. I'm sleeping here.

VOICE	Where's my Winchester?
GIRL	How should I know?
VOICE	Did my mother take it?
GIRL	Where have you been?
VOICE	I'll be right back.
GIRL	Have you been with the Rump's Daughter?
VOICE	I got to get my Winchester.
GIRL	Have you been with the Rump's Daughter?
VOICE	I'll go wake my mother.
GIRL	Answer me!
VOICE	What?
GIRL	I'm your wife now. Your only wife.
VOICE	White Girl, I was with your brother.
GIRL	You weren't with the Rump's Daughter?
VOICE	We were in jail.
GIRL	Jail?
VOICE	That sergeant over at Duck Lake, he threw us in the guard house.
GIRL	But you went for treaty money.
VOICE	Well the sergeant has it now. Somebody told them that cow I shot belonged to somebody.
GIRL	You're all wet. Here. Get warm.
VOICE	Hey girl, I been swimming.
GIRL	You got away.
VOICE	In the freezing Saskatchewan.
GIRL	What about Young Dust?
VOICE	He said it was warm there.

GIRL	You shouldn't have left him there. They threw you in jail for killing that cow.
VOICE	That cow belonged to the Great White Mother. This half-breed told me the guard said no way would I rot in jail like my dirty chief of a father. The guard said I'd hang for killing that cow!
GIRL	But that's crazy. They don't hang people over meat.
VOICE	I'm not going back to that guard house, White Girl.
GIRL	They can't take you there.
VOICE	They always come after you. My dad's in jail at Prince Albert over the pieces of a plough. He hates their stupid farming, this stupid reserve. They even turn the prairie into a jail.
GIRL	They can't put the wind in prison.
VOICE	Sounding Sky used to mean warrior. Now it's hard labour.
GIRL	Here. Dry yourself. Get warm.
VOICE	But I got to go get my Winchester.
GIRL	You rest while I find you your Winchester. They can't cross the river so quick. And you need to take some of that beef with you.
VOICE	They'll catch me with it.
GIRL	You got to eat. And the Mounties aren't going to catch us.
VOICE	But you can't come.
GIRL	I'm coming with my husband.
VOICE	You'll slow me down.
GIRL	No I won't.
VOICE	But there's snow coming.
GIRL	Better for us. Two can be warmer than one. You know that. Lie down. Lie down, John Baptist. I'll get your Winchester.
VOICE	But White Girl, crazy one—

GIRL   Lie down, John Baptist, rest. I'll be ready soon. No, rest. Listen, John Baptist, I'm a better shot than your mother Spotted Calf. I got better eyes.

VOICE   This is crazy, girl.

GIRL   Both of us. Remember?

SCENE FIVE

The projected title: "Scene Five: The Killing." ALMIGHTY VOICE and WHITE GIRL sit by the third fire. A drifting beat comes and goes on the drum.

GIRL   It's all gone. The beef's all gone.

VOICE   I don't really like beef.

GIRL   What's wrong? I didn't burn it.

VOICE   No. Cattle aren't like real meat. They're stupid.

GIRL   They're not buffalo.

VOICE   That's for sure. They don't taste right.

GIRL   I like it. It makes me feel full.

VOICE   I'll get something else soon. My wife's not going hungry.

GIRL   It's good to be hungry.

VOICE   It's better to be full.

GIRL   It reminds you you're alive. That's what my mother used to say.

VOICE   What's wrong?

GIRL   Young Dust said the snow was too deep. The treaty agent wouldn't send the supplies out. Last winter. My mother wouldn't eat. She wouldn't eat. While I was away at that school. She used to like the way I cook.

VOICE   I do too, White Girl.

GIRL   I would have cooked for her.

VOICE   Cook for me now, White Girl.

GIRL   I didn't really want to be there. We had to eat this mush made
                out of grass seeds.

VOICE   No meat?

GIRL   Mush.

VOICE   How about some tea then? It's hot enough. It'll make you feel full.

GIRL   That's all there is.

VOICE   Can we go see your father now? He likes his tea. He always
                has sugar.

GIRL   The ice was almost too thick this morning. I was afraid we'd
                have to melt snow.

VOICE   We better go soon.

GIRL   Snow takes too long.

VOICE   That sergeant's not as stupid as he looks. He'll see we
                doubled back.

GIRL   Do you know what glass is? Like thin ice?

VOICE   What are you talking about, White Girl?

GIRL   Some of the walls at the school were made out of it.

VOICE   Made out of what?

GIRL   Glass. A wall you can see through. I didn't know it was there
                at first, the wall. I tried to crawl through. I saw the sky, the
                grass moving. Out there. I banged my face. The glass broke.
                Sharp pieces, too. That's what this is from.

VOICE   A place to kiss.

GIRL   You know what, John Baptist? I dreamed about you. I knew
                you would come.

VOICE   What's the matter?

GIRL   I was looking at you far away. Through a glass wall!

VOICE   The soldiers, they have these clear beads they look through.
                Far away comes real close. All the walking in between seems
                to disappear.

GIRL	It was like that. It was. But it was also like I was waiting in my father's teepee. I could see you coming, I saw the moonlight on the barrel of your Winchester.
VOICE	I was bringing meat, I bet, buffalo meat for my wife.
GIRL	No you weren't. No! Let go.
VOICE	What's the matter, White Girl?
GIRL	You shot and the teepee broke. All the sharp pieces fell down on you, worse than hail. I think it hurt you, I think you got hurt.
VOICE	Stop it, White Girl, stop it. Don't be afraid. I'm all right.
GIRL	That god. That god. I'm afraid.
VOICE	That stupid god can't hurt me. That god belongs in that place, in the school. You're here now, I'm here now. He's not.
GIRL	He's everywhere!
VOICE	I told you he's a lie.
GIRL	He's like the glass. He's hard. He cuts you down.
VOICE	I'm your husband now. I won't let him hurt you. He doesn't deserve you.
GIRL	I'm sorry. I'm sorry.
VOICE	Listen, crazy one. You married Almighty Voice, who's not afraid to say his name. Let your glass god hear it. Almighty Voice!—who has listened to our fathers and heard what they say. Almighty Voice, who remembers our Creator and our people's ways. Almighty Voice knows how to fight for you. Do you hear what I'm saying? Do you?
GIRL	Yes. Yes, I do.
VOICE	Who is saying it?
GIRL	Almighty Voice.
VOICE	Remember who you are. Remember what your mother taught you.
GIRL	Almighty Voice, the husband of White Girl!
VOICE	I'll break your glass god for you.

GIRL	Keep your bad medicine!
VOICE	It's just a bad smell. A stink. Come on. I'll get the horse. Your father has the tea ready for us.
GIRL	Husband, look!
VOICE	Give me my Winchester. My wife'll have rabbit for breakfast.

He loads and exits. WHITE GIRL watches him go, then builds up the fire. She hears a noise from another direction and looks and stops. A shot. She runs toward the place where ALMIGHTY VOICE exited. He enters, dead rabbit in hand.

(laughing) Look how fat! This'll make you full.

GIRL	Husband, be quiet.

ALMIGHTY VOICE drops the rabbit.

It's the god. See his glass eye.

VOICE	It's the sergeant, White Girl. Just the stupid sergeant. What's he say?
GIRL	I can't understand him.
VOICE	That's that stupid half-breed with him. Stay behind me, girl.
GIRL	He wants to make peace. There's the sign.
VOICE	Get down. He's got a gun.
GIRL	Where's the half-breed going?
VOICE	Stay where you are!
GIRL	What about the horse?
VOICE	No time. Stay there! Where's the other one?
GIRL	I can't see. Over there.
VOICE	Circling around. Don't come any closer. *(He reloads his Winchester.)*
GIRL	Leave us alone! Go away!
VOICE	I'm warning you!
GIRL	Husband—

VOICE	This gun's loaded!
GIRL	—the half-breed's behind us.
VOICE	Keep close. I'm warning you! Stop there! Stay there! *(shooting)* You stupid!
GIRL	One shot. One shot, Almighty Voice!
VOICE	The other one?
GIRL	I told you glass breaks.
VOICE	Gone. Scared his horse, too. He'll bring more Mounties. There will be more from now on.
GIRL	Glass breaks so easily.
VOICE	Wife, look at me.
GIRL	I'm all right, husband.
VOICE	Come on.
GIRL	No. There will be more from now on. I'll slow you down.
VOICE	I can't leave you, girl.
GIRL	They won't hurt me. They'll be afraid to now.
VOICE	White Girl, look at me.
GIRL	They'll have to take me home. I'll tell everyone how it happened, how he wouldn't listen. They'll just take me home. I'll just slow them down. We can meet at my mother's—I mean your mother's house. My mother's gone. She died of hunger last winter. But I'm all right, Almighty Voice. And I know I have to go talk to your mother soon.
VOICE	What about?
GIRL	I want us to make her a grandchild. She has to tell me how to get ready. Women's stuff. I know I have to eat. *(She goes and picks up the rabbit.)* You better go now.

ALMIGHTY VOICE exits. WHITE GIRL takes the rabbit to the fire.

SCENE SIX

The projected title: "Scene Six: Mid-Winter Moon." A martial beat on the drum as the bloody moon rises. Then silence. WHITE GIRL sits near the second fire while ALMIGHTY VOICE wanders between the fires.

GIRL Mister. Mister! Mister God! I see your glass eye. Eye-eye! Stinky breath. It's me. Marrie! Marrie, your wife. Wife wife wife! God, look at me like before. How they taught me at school. How how. Here's my hair. Look. Here's my skin. How how, husband god, see what a little girl I am. Great White God of the ghost men, mother is here. Blood blood blood between my thighs. Yes, gimme, gimme, gimme something sweet. Oh yes, yes, you're rotten, rotten meat, but wifey wife will eat you up. Mister God, god, stupid god, this is what you want! Come on! Come on, don't leave! I'm your little squaw. Eye-eye! See! Eye-eye, Mister God. Eye-eye!

VOICE Don't talk, cousin. You're being stupid. No one would mistake you for a warrior. And your woman, she's so skinny, no one would call you a hunter either. Or a lover. Could your woman do what my woman has? Could she look those white men in the eyes? They took her back to Duck Lake and kept her in that guard house and she gave them lies for their lies. "Run, husband. We will meet later." She said that to me. Is it a surprise I think about her? I believe what she says. If she is crazy, we all should be. Not a word, Little Salteau! Who's the one who killed a Mountie?

GIRL I am the wife of Almighty Voice. You don't know my name. You don't even wonder if I have one. I'm only a crazy squaw. You're watching me but you expect to see my husband. His is a name you know. Almighty Voice. John Baptist. You say these names of his over and over again, like the prayers you say to your glass-eyed god for the grace of your Great White Mother Victoria. But your prayers won't make him come. Mister God Mountie, you don't know what his name means.

17

VOICE   Your sister, Young Dust, she makes me remember how my father used to talk about the buffalo. Maybe because she likes meat so much. I'd like to feed her till she's fat. My father said everyone used to be like that. Everyone used to follow the buffalo. He hates farming. A man shouldn't be a bag of bones. My mother says he gets no meat. In Prince Albert. John Sounding Sky is in jail because his son mistook a Mountie for a cow!

GIRL   You're laughing with that half-breed. "Let the crazy squaw go home. Easy to keep an eye on her there." So he unlocks the door, walks away to the fire where you play with your silver coin, your dollar. That's what you want to trade my husband's blood for. Why? What is its power? A coin is not the moon. Can't you see it's dead, Mister Mountie? Cold as the bullet my husband kills rabbits or enemies with.

VOICE   So my mother Spotted Calf is alone still, running things, hating it. She says there are too many women now. I think there aren't enough men. It's like a war but no one will say so, so there's never any peace. How many of our brothers are there still in Stoney Mountain? How many come home in the spring? My mother says it makes her children crazy, living on snow. Maybe she's right. Come on. Let's go make some blood flow tonight!

GIRL   You've got a bad look on your face, a blindness, a glassy gaze. What are you staring at? Your silver dollar? The fire? My husband's bullet. You'll stare till they all turn to glass. And what will you see through them then? That forever place you want to live, the one they promised me in school? I turn here in the wind toward the river and the moon is there, a woman with better things to do. She slips away from you, going home.

SCENE SEVEN

The projected title: "Scene Seven: Honeymoon." The drum beats. The full moon sweeps down from the sky like a spotlight to show and surround the lovers, lying together on the ground.

GIRL   Almighty Voice, come on.

VOICE   Not again.

GIRL   I want to be sure.

VOICE   Let me sleep.

GIRL   This is the time to do it. Your mother said so.

VOICE   I don't want to know that. I don't want to do it for my mother.

GIRL   Do it for me. It's the best time now.

VOICE   I don't want to know that stuff.

GIRL   Young Dust dreamed we had a son.

VOICE   This is none of your brother's business.

GIRL   Come on, John Baptist.

VOICE   White Girl, we got to sleep.

GIRL   Almighty Voice, do you like my hand there?

VOICE   Don't. You keep this up, we'll fall asleep on the horse later.

GIRL   You fall off, you can fall on me.

VOICE   White Girl, we got to move on tonight. Little Salteau said those stupid Mounties are just south of here.

GIRL   They're hunting quail, not us. I like it here. I like how flat it is. Like your belly.

VOICE   White Girl, stop it.

GIRL   Come on, Almighty Voice.

VOICE	Do as your husband says. And don't laugh.
GIRL	The Mounties don't know we're here. Why worry?
VOICE	Go to sleep.
GIRL	They'll forget about you.
VOICE	I killed a Mountie. They don't give up.
GIRL	But he would have killed you.
VOICE	I know.
GIRL	Spring comes, the snow goes. Too many other things to do. Cows running away through the grass. Fresh meat, husband.
VOICE	Can't you be quiet, girl?
GIRL	Isn't this grass moving in the wind here on your flat prairie?
VOICE	I'm your husband, White Girl.
GIRL	Oh, your wife likes to run in the grass, Almighty Voice.
VOICE	Stop it. Go to sleep.
GIRL	They can't see you as long as you're with me.
VOICE	We can't hide in that grass, little girl.
GIRL	We can hide. With me you're in the dark of the moon. It's what your mother talks about. When we're together, it's like we're inside a bead of glass made of wind. They can't get at us. It's my medicine, husband. In the dream—you were in the dream. That's all I can tell you.
VOICE	You fasted? When?
GIRL	The last blizzard. Your mother took me out. In that wind.
VOICE	The moon was dark then.
GIRL	She took me down to the river. I built a fire on the ice. She visited me every morning. And she sang to me.
VOICE	And she serves tea to the priest!
GIRL	And laughs at him. He expects her to give you away. That priest wants her to marry his god too.

VOICE   That's crazy.

GIRL   Instead she gets news of your father in Prince Albert.

VOICE   I didn't know. What does she say about my father? Is his cough any better? When One Arrow got back from the jail at Stoney Mountain, he was old. He told my father that the visions of warriors have no more power against the soldiers.

GIRL   He was old, husband. He was tired.

VOICE   Not even Riel's vision, and he was part white.

GIRL   It's the jail, husband. They watch you all the time. You can't move.

VOICE   I was there when he said it.

GIRL   And it's all stone.

VOICE   He gave away his rifle.

GIRL   You can't see anything but stones. You can't see anything, husband. You forget everything.

VOICE   How can you forget everything and be a man?

GIRL   You're not a man then. You're like a ghost. You're lost.

VOICE   I want to see my father. I'm going to Prince Albert.

GIRL   That's crazy.

VOICE   The Mounties won't know I'm there. Why worry?

GIRL   Your mother says someone's always watching him. You don't know that place.

VOICE   I'm going to talk to him.

GIRL   You have to hide. Your mother said so.

VOICE   Shut up about my mother! I don't want to hear it.

GIRL   She won't let you go.

VOICE   Am I a child again? Hiding behind women. How can you look at me?

GIRL   You're my husband.

VOICE	My father is a man. John Sounding Sky still means warrior. But Almighty Voice?
GIRL	He's a warrior.
VOICE	Does a warrior run away? Almighty Voice is a stupid old man, a ghost. He's here, there, nowhere.
GIRL	You can't go.
VOICE	I should be in Prince Albert. John Sounding Sky should be at home with Spotted Calf.
GIRL	They ache to hang Almighty Voice.
VOICE	What good am I here?
GIRL	I need you.
VOICE	What good am I to you, White Girl?
GIRL	I don't want to be alone.
VOICE	You can stay with my mother.
GIRL	Two women old with no men? Your mother will die like my mother did. You can't leave me too.
VOICE	Your father will take you.
GIRL	You're sending me home?
VOICE	He'll get you a better husband.
GIRL	He'll get me a worse one.
VOICE	Who? Who could that be?
GIRL	Any ghost man will do. You want me to die.
VOICE	You won't die!
GIRL	I will. For years. Kill me now. Be good to me, husband. Kill me now and then you can go, go and be hanged.
VOICE	You're pretty fierce, all right.
GIRL	Let go of me.
VOICE	For a little girl.

GIRL   I'll get you your Winchester.

VOICE   Stay here with me.

GIRL   You can kill me, husband. We'll both be dead.

VOICE   That's stupid. White Girl who has visions, stay here with me.

GIRL   What about your father?

VOICE   We'll find a way. My mother will help.

GIRL   You won't leave me?

VOICE   Hey, I'm here with you. In the dark of the moon. They can't get at us.

GIRL   Almighty Voice—

VOICE   Can't you be quiet, girl? Your husband doesn't want to sleep anymore. He likes your hand here.

SCENE EIGHT

A projected title: "Scene Eight: The Hunting Moon." A gunshot. The social drum. Three more shots. ALMIGHTY VOICE with his Winchester at the last fire, the dead one. WHITE GIRL with a baby-sized bundle in her arms, still illuminated by the moon.

GIRL   You brought me home to your mother. It was time. Spotted Calf expected me. She took me into her new house. Other women were waiting. "Go away," she said. "Young Dust will bring you news." Someone, the Rump's Daughter, might tell. It was dangerous. The Mounties—it was dangerous. You wanted to hide under the floor, under her bed like last winter. But she made you go. "You men shouldn't know women's stuff." You men. Little Salteau and Dubling came along. I heard you laughing. Off you rode to hunt somewhere, the grass new, blue-green. I saw you through the glass in the window of that house. Going.

VOICE   Has he come? Tell him, wife, tell him how good a season it was everywhere along the Saskatchewan the winter before he was born. Tell him I always found game, never got cold. Till now. Say the ghost men shivered in their huts, too afraid of the wind to fire a shot. Tell him it can be like that again. Tell him, girl. Do you hear me? I wish you did.

Tell him how we visited and people would give his mother more to eat. Even people in the woods far up north. An old bull buffalo, chewy but sweet. You worried it might be their last one but ate anyway. Tell him Old Dust gave in, gave us lots of sugar for our tea, called me son, when he saw how fat you were. One day I remember. Cold, bright. Leather stiff as wood. Your belly had begun to curve. Your breath feathers, or smoke that fell, hugged the ground. I teased you, your belly like the iron stove at the store at Duck Lake. Tight as a drum. I felt him kick then. What a thump! I knew I had a son. I wanted to dance.

> *ALMIGHTY VOICE dances with the drum in celebration. Then, as WHITE GIRL speaks, his steps turn into a war dance and then into stillness. The moon around WHITE GIRL turns bloody.*

GIRL They tell me you came across another cow. They say you wanted to feast me and the baby. So you shot the stupid thing. Some farmer heard your guns, didn't mind his own business. Him and his sons gave chase. I can hear you laughing, leading them into this bluff of poplars. And suddenly there's Mounties, soldiers, farmers everywhere. And someone shoots someone. I hope it was that farmer. They tell me you got no food, no water all day. They say someone else got shot. Maybe a Mountie. Young Dust said he heard you singing. War songs. He says you were dancing. There were ghost men all around that night. Farmers, soldiers, priests of the glass god. Over a hundred against Little Salteau, Dubling, and Almighty Voice by the end. And two big iron guns. I saw them myself the second day. Spotted Calf and I stood watching. I wanted you to be anywhere else. Young Dust held the baby, reminded me to feed his nephew. I didn't notice I was full, aching. I have no milk now. *(She puts her bundle down.)* That night I saw my husband Almighty Voice again against that moon I had tried to forget. Then those two guns started firing and firing. Firing and firing. It was cold and the smoke would not go away. I seemed to see you sometime in the night, in the smoke, but even before morning broke, your mother was singing her death song.

SCENE NINE

A projected title: "Scene Nine: His Vision." The drum beats in the night. The moon is low in the sky, pulsing. ALMIGHTY VOICE lies by the dead fire, his leg badly wounded. The spectral teepee appears and the drum goes silent. Inside the teepee are WHITE GIRL and her baby, mother and child, a destination. ALMIGHTY VOICE rises and uses his Winchester as a crutch to come to the teepee. WHITE GIRL comes out and shows him the baby and the baby cries. The moon turns white. ALMIGHTY VOICE dies.

ACT TWO

A follow spot finds a title placard: "Act Two: Ghost Dance."

The spot shifts to a second title placard: "Scene One: Overture,"
then fades. Spectral light from the dead fire. ALMIGHTY
VOICE, now in whiteface as his own GHOST, continues his
dance of celebration around the fire inside the last crescent of the
moon. Scattered around the moon's half-circle are ruined stools, three
of which are still sturdy enough to be useful. On the one upright at
the crescent's midpoint, a searching spot finds a seated figure and,
finding its head, discovers white-gloved hands hiding its face. As the
crescent moon fades, the hands open to reveal the whiteface that
masks WHITE GIRL into the role of the
INTERLOCUTOR, a Mountie and the Master of Ceremonies.
In a glance their eyes meet. Sudden light shift to variety-show lights,
both the GHOST and the INTERLOCUTOR in follow spots.
The INTERLOCUTOR adjusts her monocle.

INTERLOCUTOR

Here, here? I said, "Here, here." Hey dead man! Hey red man!
Hey Indian!

GHOST   *Awas. Si-pwete. [Go away. Go on.]*

INTERLOCUTOR

"Here, here," I said. What's the meaning of this? Come on,
use the queen's tongue, or I'll sell you to a cigar store.

GHOST   *Awas kititin ni-nimihiton oma ota. [Go away. I'm dancing here.]*

INTERLOCUTOR

You dare call these furtive foot steps, these frenzied flailings
of arms like wings, dancing! Stop it. It's nonsense.

GHOST   *Awena kiya? Kekwiy ka-ayimota-man? [Who are you? What are*
you talking about?]

INTERLOCUTOR

Snap out of it, Chief. *(slapping him with the gloves four times)*

GHOST   Oweeya! Oweeya! Ya! Ya! *Pakitinin awena kiya moya ki-kis-ke yimitin. [Ow! Ow! Ow! Ow! Let go of me. Who are you? I don't know you.]*

INTERLOCUTOR

You know very well who the hell I am. I don't have to remind you no show can begin without its master. Here, here. Stop I say. How dare you go faster.

GHOST   *Nahkee. Kawiya-(ekosi). Ponikawin poko ta kisisimoyan. [Stop. Let me alone. I have to finish my dance.]*

INTERLOCUTOR

I'll break the other leg for you, Kisse-Manitou-Wayou.

GHOST   *Tansi esi kiskeyitaman ni wiyowin? [How do you know my name?]*

INTERLOCUTOR

Names, names, they're all the same. Crees all wear feathers. Dead man, red man, Indian, Kisse-Manitou-Wayou, Almighty Voice, John Baptist! Geronimo, Tonto, Calijah. Or most simply, Mister Ghost.

GHOST   Ghost?

INTERLOCUTOR

Boo! Almighty Ghost, Chief. Now we're speaking English.

GHOST   What? Who are you?

INTERLOCUTOR

How. You're supposed to say "How." You know. Hey Pontiac, how's the engine? Can't you stick to the script? You're too new at this ghost schtick to go speaking *ad liberatum.*

GHOST   Let me go. I don't know you. Let me dance.

INTERLOCUTOR

Here here. Stop, I say. How dare you! Do I have to remind you this colourful display, these exotic ceremonials, belong later on in the program? Listen to me, Chief. One doesn't begin with a climax, an end. Unmitigated foolishness, I'll have you know. If you begin at the end, then where do you go? Do you know? No. Well? What have you got to say for yourself?

GHOST   How—

INTERLOCUTOR

That's more like it!

GHOST   How did I get here? What's going on?

INTERLOCUTOR

What's going on! The show. The Red and White Victoria
Regina Spirit Revival show! These fine, kind folks want to
know the truth, the amazing details and circumstance behind
your savagely beautiful appearance. They also want to be
entertained and enlightened and maybe a tiny bit thrilled,
just a goose of frightened. They want to laugh and cry. They
want to know the facts. And it's up to you and me to try and
lie that convincingly. And since all the rest of our company
is late for the curtain, this is your chance, your big break for
certain.

GHOST   No, I won't dance for you.

INTERLOCUTOR

But you have to toe the line, Chief. We all do. Here. Let me
smell your breath. Bah! Like death warmed over. I've warned
you before. You choose to booze and you're back on the
street where I found you.

GHOST   Leave me alone. Go away.

INTERLOCUTOR

Don't you realize you could be internationally known, the
most acclaimed magic act of the century?

GHOST   What do you mean?

INTERLOCUTOR

The Vanishing Indian!

GHOST   Poof?

INTERLOCUTOR

Forget about faggots.

GHOST   I want to know how I got here.

INTERLOCUTOR

Gutter. Does that sound mean anything to you? Gutter?

GHOST   All I remember—

INTERLOCUTOR
Answer me, you sotted fancy dancer.

GHOST   My leg was gone.

INTERLOCUTOR
Come on, Chief, be a friend.

GHOST   It was! I used a branch from a sapling.

INTERLOCUTOR
Be a pal, Chiefy, dear.

GHOST   No, it was my gun for a crutch.

INTERLOCUTOR
This is a bit much for this early in the proceedings.

GHOST   Sometime in the night—

INTERLOCUTOR
Wait wait wait. I'd like to apologize to the ladies in the
audience and suggest that this might be a prime opportunity
to make use of our theatre's other facilities. The details of the
following story may be not for the faint of heart, are in fact
quite gory, and ordinarily it would be our custom to warn
you and ask your permission before we proceed. However—
how-ever—as you can see, my peer here feels he must thrust
the entire tale upon us. Once again, I apologize. Thank you
for your attention. All right. Proceed.

GHOST   My legs were gone.

INTERLOCUTOR
His leg was gone!

GHOST   I must have screamed.

INTERLOCUTOR
Talk about Wounded Knee.

GHOST   But my throat was too dry.

INTERLOCUTOR
The bones were shattered, pulp. Not that that mattered.

GHOST   There was no sound in my mouth.

INTERLOCUTOR
Quite the comedown for Almighty Vocal Cords.

GHOST
I couldn't sing my song.

INTERLOCUTOR
Oh Lord, talented, too!

GHOST
My death song. I crawled out of the pit.

INTERLOCUTOR
And we're not talking orchestra pits out here in the sticks.

GHOST
We had dug it in the ground to protect us from the gunfire.

INTERLOCUTOR
Not much good compared to a couple of cannons, was it?

GHOST
There was smoke close to the ground.

INTERLOCUTOR
From the fires all around?

GHOST
I thought I might be able to make it across the open space.

INTERLOCUTOR
And was it really over a hundred men by then?

GHOST
Against Little Salteau, Dubling, and me.

INTERLOCUTOR
Imagine. Red coats and wild Indians. What a spectacle! Where are my glasses?

GHOST
It was the middle of the night. I might get by if the watch was asleep.

INTERLOCUTOR
Not on duty? Now that's not very funny.

GHOST
I had seen her watching, many times that day, beyond their lines. I got halfway across.

INTERLOCUTOR
And amazingly, no one saw him then. He might have made good his escape. Think about that. However—how-ever—he was bleeding a lot. Red blood oozing from red skin. Oh what a thrill! I'm not offending you, am I?

GHOST   She came to meet me.

INTERLOCUTOR
(à la "Indian Love Call") When I'm calling you-oo-oo-oo-oo-oo-oo!

GHOST   No one could see her. My wife had denied their glass-eyed god. It was her medicine to be invisible.

INTERLOCUTOR
Wish my wife could do that. That's really interesting. Kissy Kisse-Manitou-Wayou? Did you give her some tongue!

GHOST   She told me about my son. She told me I would not be forgotten.

INTERLOCUTOR
How can I put this delicately? Your last meeting, your last touch. Your life dribbling out of you, hot and sticky. Big strong buck like you used to be. Was it savage love? Did you have a last quickie?

GHOST   I knew I could die then.

INTERLOCUTOR
She was some babe, eh?

GHOST   People would remember me.

INTERLOCUTOR
Give me some of the juicy details, Chief.

GHOST   My people would remember me.

INTERLOCUTOR
One must always strive for accuracy. Do you have documentation?

GHOST   I knew I could die then.

INTERLOCUTOR
Come on, Chief, speak up. Anybody got a cigar? Never mind.

GHOST   I could hear my mother, off on the hill, singing her song.

INTERLOCUTOR
Talent just runs in that family!

GHOST   Her death song.

INTERLOCUTOR

So does manic depression! Do we feel better now? We do remember you, Mister Almighty Ghost. The angry young man, the passionate lover, the wild and crazy Indian kid. A shocking but true tale of the frontier. Now don't you think this is just too touching, ladies and gentlemen? Too much for my refined sensibilities, that's a certainty. That wasn't too bad, Chief, considering. And now— *(She changes the title placard.)*

SCENE TWO

The new placard reads "Scene Two: Baritone Solo."

INTERLOCUTOR

Ladies and gentlemen, for your further edification and delight, a musical selection. Mister Almighty Ghost, the famous Aboriginal voice, will now render for you the sweet ballad, "Lament of the Redskin Lover." Mister Ghost?

GHOST   *(in a spotlight)* What are you talking about?

INTERLOCUTOR

Go on, Mister Ghost. We wait upon you, sir. Sing. Sing.

GHOST   I don't know this.

INTERLOCUTOR

No memory at all? Here. It's number two on your lyric sheet, sir.

GHOST   Who are you?

INTERLOCUTOR

This is it, your last show. You're back on the street in the morning. The gutter? Here we go.

> *The INTERLOCUTOR stands behind the GHOST and guides him through the accompanying mime.*

GHOST   *(to the tune of "Oh! Susanna")*

I track the winter prairie for the little squaw I lost.
I'm missing all the kissing I had afore the frost.
I'm moping, oh I'm hoping oh, to hold her hand in mine.
My flower of Saskatchewan, oh we were doing fine.

GHOST & INTERLOCUTOR

In our teepee, oh we were so in love,
One Arrow was too narrow for my little squaw and me.

GHOST   I had a dream the other night, I saw her on a hill.

INTERLOCUTOR

My little squaw was shaking, the wind was standing still.

GHOST   The bannock bread was in her mouth, and
blood was in her eye.
The moon so bright I lost my sight—

INTERLOCUTOR

—I pray she didn't die!

GHOST   On the prairie, oh how the white does blow!
Who makes it through the winter?
Not my little squaw or me.

INTERLOCUTOR

Nicely done. Thank you, thank you, Mister Ghost. You were almost your spooky self again.

GHOST   Thank you, Mister Interlocutor.

INTERLOCUTOR

Buck up, Mister Ghost. Isn't this all familiar? Might not, say, Buck and Squaw be the latest dance craze?

> *The INTERLOCUTOR pulls the GHOST into a short Hollywood Indian War Dance. The GHOST resists. At the end the GHOST grabs the INTERLOCUTOR and looks into her eyes.*

GHOST   This is what they've done to you.

INTERLOCUTOR

Thank you, thank you, Mister Ghost. A most original interpretation of the material. Gentle listeners, Mister Bones will now perform for you—

GHOST   Mister Bones? He the one with the dice?

INTERLOCUTOR
No, Mister Ghost. He's the one who's got rhythm.

GHOST   There's no one like that backstage, sir.

INTERLOCUTOR
No? Perhaps our friend Mister Tambo waits in the wings.

GHOST   That the Tamborine Man? Not even in the flies, sir. Nor, sir, is Mister Drum lurking below the trap door.

INTERLOCUTOR
No Mister Drum? Well, Mister Ghost—no! Wait!

The GHOST changes the placard.

SCENE THREE

The new placard reads "Scene Three: The Stump."

GHOST   Ladies and gentlemen, boys and girls, dogs and cats, we of the Pale-Faced Band of the Sweet Saskatchewaners are pleased to present for your information and concern our own Mister Interlocutor in the role of Mister Drum, a loyal citizen of our territory.

INTERLOCUTOR
Wait a moment, Mister Ghost. That is not my part.

GHOST   But you do know it by heart. This is your chance, sir, your big break for certain. Ladies and gentlemen, please welcome Mister Drum.

INTERLOCUTOR
Ahem. Ahem. I come before you this evening, my dear friends, full, full of concern. We have ourselves a problem, dear friends, an Indian problem. Dare I say an indigent Indian problem? Dear friends, the pampered redskins, they are the bad ones. Those tribes that have been cared for as if they were our equals, they, dear friends, are the first to turn and shed the blood of their benefactors. Noisemaker was

petted, yes, even feted, my friends, and now raids our farms. Pricky Pinecone was paid to come up to our fine territory and what, dear friends, is his pursuit nowadays? Carnage! Large Prairie Dog, who for years has sharpened his teeth by chewing on the bone of idleness, shows his gratitude by killing his priests for their holy wine. That is not communion, friends. Little Dump, a non-treaty Indian, has been, friends, provisioned with all necessaries and so gets to spend all his days gallivanting about the territory, shouting loudly and plotting mischief. And now, my dear friends, this Almighty Gas character joins in on the season's carnival of ruin. Oh friends, the petted Indians have proved the bad ones and this gives weight to the wise adage, friends, that the only good Indians are the dead ones.

GHOST   Bravo! Bravo, Mister Interlocutor, sir. Mister Drum could not have said it better.

INTERLOCUTOR
Thank you, Mister Ghost.

GHOST   No, thank you, Mister Interlocutor. I take your words to heart. My heart soars! We all thank you, sir. Don't we, ladies and gentles? Never a truer word was said. It is to our great benefit to know of this dread red threat to our well-beings and livelihoods, this deadly hood, this Almighty Fart character. Dead Indians would be even better, sir, if they didn't stink that way.

INTERLOCUTOR
Thank you again, Mister Ghost, thank you again. I thank you too, ladies and gentle sirs. We will now return to the sequence of events as listed in your programs.

GHOST   But sir, there's still no sign of Messers Bone, Tambo, Drum, or any one. The entire company, sir, seems to be running on Indian Time!

INTERLOCUTOR
Would you now consider performing, Mister Ghost, for our attentive friends, that charming curiosity you called a dance?

GHOST   No.

INTERLOCUTOR
Surely, Mister Ghost—

GHOST
Call me the late Almighty Voice. Call me an early redman. Call me, yes, even call me a ghost—but don't call me Shirley!

INTERLOCUTOR
You're the most spirited ghost I've ever met.

GHOST
You better believe it. There's a stir of dissatisfaction, sir, in the audience. Perhaps number seven?

INTERLOCUTOR
An excellent suggestion, Mister Ghost. An excellent selection, I assure you, my friends.

GHOST
But, sir, it calls for the entire company. And we, sir, are the skeleton crew!

SCENE FOUR

The INTERLOCUTOR changes the title placard to "Scene Four: The Walkaround."

INTERLOCUTOR
Ladies and gentlemen, for your delight and encouragement, Mister Ghost and Yours Truly will now present a martial interlude. In honour of all our heroic boys in uniform!

GHOST
I'll even honour those boys out of uniform.

INTERLOCUTOR
I appear first in the role of Mister Allan, leading the charge through the bluff. After the renegade!

GHOST
Hurrah! We're beating the bushes.

INTERLOCUTOR
Where are the cowards?

GHOST
Moo? Pow, pow!

INTERLOCUTOR

Ambush, vicious ambush!

GHOST It appears Mister Allan's fallen off his horse!

INTERLOCUTOR

A bullet! A bullet shattered my arm.

GHOST Bull! The bottle did him in.

INTERLOCUTOR

Then I take the part of the brave second-in-command, Mister Raven.

GHOST Already shot on the wing.

INTERLOCUTOR

What?

GHOST In his private parts!

INTERLOCUTOR

Not my leg?

GHOST Groin, groin, gone!

INTERLOCUTOR

Oh where is the rest of my happy company?

GHOST Retreat! Retreat! Buck up, my friend, there are but three of them.

INTERLOCUTOR

We've got them outnumbered. I, Mister Hockin, take charge. Surround the bluff!

GHOST But are you nine and the settlers enough?

INTERLOCUTOR

Postmaster Grundy here, volunteer, sir. We'll all of us beat them bushes again.

GHOST March then. March south, men. They can't hide from you.

INTERLOCUTOR

Where have they gone? We had them surrounded.

GHOST This could be embarrassing.

INTERLOCUTOR
    East to west now. Shoulder to shoulder.

GHOST   Nothing. No one. Again?

INTERLOCUTOR
    Here we go. These darn trees.

GHOST   Unpopular poplars?

INTERLOCUTOR
    If they weren't so green. Fire would force them out.

GHOST   Say again.

INTERLOCUTOR
    Fire!

GHOST   Bang bang! Bang bang, bang bang, bang bang! The mail
    comes late.

INTERLOCUTOR
    Why?

GHOST   Postmaster Grundy got shot in the gut.

INTERLOCUTOR
    What about Hockin?

GHOST   His heart got broken.

INTERLOCUTOR
    And Kerr?

GHOST   Sorry, sir. Retreat! Retreat!

INTERLOCUTOR
    I don't want to wait all day and all night.

GHOST   Too late.

INTERLOCUTOR
    I could have got them.

GHOST   Reinforcements arrive!

INTERLOCUTOR
    I could have got them alive!

GHOST   So can I play the one little, two little dozen Mounties?

INTERLOCUTOR
I'll take the roles of the two big guns!

GHOST   Bang bang? Boom boom. Doom doom!

INTERLOCUTOR
As well as the crowd of concerned civilians, including the disappointed—

GHOST   —I do so much for those ungrateful wretches—

INTERLOCUTOR
—farm instructor and his friend the ever hopeful—

GHOST   —Spare the rod and spoil the child!—

INTERLOCUTOR
—missionary priest. Well?

GHOST   It will be the least I can do then and an honour to represent the man's wife and mother as well as others from the One Arrow Reserve, Treaty Number Six.

INTERLOCUTOR
Perhaps, then, you will do the parts then of the young man and his ill-fated companions? Yes?

GHOST   No.

INTERLOCUTOR
Mister Ghost, sure—please listen to me and consider—

GHOST   Fuck you. I'm not going through that again for your entertainment.

INTERLOCUTOR
Mister Ghost—

GHOST   You do it.

INTERLOCUTOR
(to the tune of "Derry Down") Who is fighting the battle for everyone—

GHOST   —is fighting the battle for everyone—

INTERLOCUTOR
—fights bloodthirsty redskins and wears a grin—

GHOST   —not afeard of anything?—

GHOST & INTERLOCUTOR

> Who rides high in the saddle and shoots a gun,
> rides high in the saddle and shoots a gun,
> shoots bloodthirsty redskins and wears a grin,
> not afeard of anything?
> We have the guns, the guts, the wit.
> We know that you are stinking shit.
> We did it to the buffalo.
> Want to be next? Yes or no?
> We are the men with guns and bucks.
> We know that you are stupid fucks.
> We did it to the buffalo.
> Want to be next? Yes or no?

INTERLOCUTOR

> Who is fighting the battle for everyone,
> is fighting the battle for everyone,
> shoots bloodthirsty redskins and wears a grin,
> not afeard of anything?

GHOST   We have the guns, the guts, the wit.
> We know that you are stupid shit.
> We did it to the buffalo.
> Want to be next? Yes or no?

GHOST & INTERLOCUTOR

> We are the men,
> well let's say it again,
> to get them heathen Indians.
> We are the ones,
> oh let's do it with guns,
> let's kill them stinking Indians.
> We are the ones,
> well let's do it with rum,
> let's get them redskin Indians.
> We are the men,
> oh let's say it again,
> to kill them damn dead Indians.

GHOST   Who rides high in the saddle and shoots a gun,
> rides high in the saddle and shoots a gun,

shoots bloodthirsty redskins and wears a grin,
not afeard of anything?

INTERLOCUTOR

We have the guns, the guts, the wit.
We know that you are stinking shit.
We did it to the buffalo.
Want to be next? Yes or No?

GHOST & INTERLOCUTOR

We have the bucks and you do not.
Is it a wonder that you got shot?
We have the bucks and you do not.
Is it a wonder that you got shot?
We have the bucks and you do not.
Is it a wonder that you got shot?
We have the bucks and you do not.
Is it a wonder that you got shot?

We have the blankets and the rum.
Oh did you say that you want some?

GHOST   Well, Mister Interlocutor, how do you feel now?

INTERLOCUTOR

No, Mister Ghost, how do you feel now?

GHOST   Well, Mister Interlocutor, I feel somewhat like a newspaper.

INTERLOCUTOR

You feel like a newspaper? How is that, Mister Ghost?

GHOST   I'm pale as a sheet of paper.

INTERLOCUTOR

A sheet of paper? With black eyes, Mister Ghost?

GHOST   Every one dotted, sir.

The INTERLOCUTOR hits the GHOST.

And ultimately, sir, I am like a newspaper in that I am read
all over—the countryside.

INTERLOCUTOR

Red all over, sir? A most colourful conceit. Bloody good, as our cousins would have it. Newspapers are our pass to an understanding of the reserve and the life of its denizens.

GHOST And we don't have to go to the Indian agent to get them. The passes.

INTERLOCUTOR
Are you making one at me, sir? *(hitting him)* Did you read how we're teaching our primitive friends agriculture?

GHOST That'll bring them down to earth.

INTERLOCUTOR
And we're giving them the benefit of our modern tongue.

GHOST They'll need no other one, our kingdom come.

INTERLOCUTOR
Did you read how tranquil and subordinate they've become under our wise and humane government?

> *The GHOST claps a "gunshot."*

Was that a gun? A shot?

GHOST Likely not. The Indian agent won't give them any more ammunition until they put in a crop.

INTERLOCUTOR
What will they eat in the meantime?

GHOST *(hitting himself)* Off to the hoose-gow with them! Lazy is as lazy does. So it says in the newspaper. Or the Bible. *(reprising "Derry Down")*

Who is shooting in battle at every one,
is shooting in battle at everyone—

GHOST & INTERLOCUTOR
—fights bloodthirsty redskins and wears a grin,
not afeard of anything?—

GHOST —We have the words, the pens, the laws.
We know that treaties are for fools.
We did it to the buffalo.
You want to be next?

SCENE FIVE

The GHOST reveals the next placard: "Scene Five: Tenor Solo."

GHOST   And now, for the particular delectation of the ladies in the audience—

INTERLOCUTOR
              What are you doing?

GHOST   —Mister Interlocutor will render in his most famous transvestatory manner—

INTERLOCUTOR
              I won't do this.

GHOST   —as the Princess Porkly Haunches, he now sings "The Sioux Song."

INTERLOCUTOR
              This is not a regular part of the program, ladies and gentlemen.

GHOST   And therefore we must show our gratitude to the princess. Let us further encourage her, ladies and gentle sirs.

INTERLOCUTOR
              (to the tune of "Amazing Grace")

              How beautiful
              A man the moon.
              I am what I am.
              I'm not above
              A buck for love.
              What good is it? Sioux me.

              A sparkling place
              The city is.
              My face is my face.
              I must go far
              Below zero.
              What good is it? Sioux me.

My name is Sioux.
What did I do?
I never ever said
That red is what
I want to drink.
It goes right to my head.

How beautiful
A place the past.
We are where we are.
The redskin race
Finishes last.
What good is it? Sioux me.

GHOST   Thank you, thank you, Mister Interlocutor. An astonishingly touching masquerade. It seemed almost real. Is this a tear here, washing the war paint?

INTERLOCUTOR
Unhand me, sir. I'm not afraid of you.

GHOST   Boo is no go then. So how do you feel, Mister Interlocutor?

INTERLOCUTOR
I'm the Interlocutor here!

GHOST   How do you feel now?

INTERLOCUTOR
I know what to do. I know the order of the show.

GHOST   You do, do you?

INTERLOCUTOR
I want my happy company.

GHOST   They're even later than I am, sir. It's curtains for all of us!

INTERLOCUTOR
No, the show must go on.

GHOST   The audience is waiting. Mister Interlocutor?

INTERLOCUTOR
The playlet.

SCENE SIX

The INTERLOCUTOR reveals the placard: "Scene Six: The Playlet."

GHOST　　The playlet!

INTERLOCUTOR
　　　　Ladies and gentlemen, as a public service to the citizens at the forefront of our civilization, we now present a short drama of spiritual significance.

GHOST　　Mister Interlocutor, in the continued absence of Mister Bones, will now render the role of Sweet Sioux.

INTERLOCUTOR
　　　　I dream. I dream, I do, of the bright lights of the city. Regina, she's the finest, the queen city of my dreams. But I promised Daddy, Daddy dear, I would keep up the homestead, I would be his little red pioneer. This on his deathbed. Sigh. Gangrene from an arrow. Oh horror!

GHOST　　Shot by me, ha ha, in error. Oops!

INTERLOCUTOR
　　　　Mister Ghost now appears, in the infelicitous absence of Mister Tambo, in the role of the villainous Chief Magistrate.

GHOST　　Ahem. Ahem. Give me some rum or I'll shoot you in the bum. I need firewater for a starter. Then off I go on a hunt or to court. Order, order, I say to the buffalo. Right between the eyes, I warn the prisoners. Tonight it's too late, too late for her.

INTERLOCUTOR
　　　　It is the eleventh hour. It is beyond my power to pay the mortgage on my daddy's farm. Oh I am losing courage.

GHOST　　Knocka knocka, Sweet Sioux.

INTERLOCUTOR

Who's there? At this hour.

GHOST   Knocka knocka.

INTERLOCUTOR

What would Daddy do?

GHOST   Answer the door.

INTERLOCUTOR

You think so?

GHOST   Knocka knocka, Sioux!

INTERLOCUTOR

Hello. Who's there?

GHOST   It is I, my dear. Your sweetheart, Chief Magistrate.

INTERLOCUTOR

You're no sweetheart to me.

GHOST   She's not all there up here. Sometimes she believes me.

INTERLOCUTOR

Stay away. What is it you want?

GHOST   The time is short. The deed on this land is about to come
due. I was worried, my dear, about you.

INTERLOCUTOR

You were? Really?

GHOST   Do you have the necessary dollars?

INTERLOCUTOR

No—

GHOST   —Hooray!—

INTERLOCUTOR

—I'm sorry to say.

GHOST   I mean to say 'I'm here to help you.

INTERLOCUTOR

But at what price? A chief doesn't become magistrate
without vice.

GHOST   Oh Sweet Sioux.

INTERLOCUTOR
              What's a girl to do?

GHOST   Oh sweet Sweet Sioux.

INTERLOCUTOR
              Oh, no, Chief Magistrate. I couldn't do that.

GHOST   Why not, my dear? She's done it before.

INTERLOCUTOR
              I'm not that kind of girl. I only do it for love and/or
              marriage.

GHOST   Why buy the moo cow?

INTERLOCUTOR
              I won't do it for meat anymore.

GHOST   I'll give the deed to you.

INTERLOCUTOR
              Oh no. I couldn't do that. That would make me one of those
              women, nothing more than a squaw.

GHOST   A squaw? You mean like Buck and Squaw?

              *The GHOST pulls the INTERLOCUTOR into a reprise of
              the Hollywood Indian War Dance. The INTERLOCUTOR
              complies but keeps it short.*

INTERLOCUTOR
              Midnight is about to strike!

GHOST   There goes the farm.

INTERLOCUTOR
              But I keep my honour.

GHOST   Midnight strikes. The farm is mine. And what the hell, so are
              you!

INTERLOCUTOR
              Oh no no! That would be—rape!

GHOST   Right you are! You're more intelligent than you appear.

INTERLOCUTOR

Rape, oh no!

GHOST

Oh yes, yes, Sweet Sioux! Talk about the Almighty Buck.

INTERLOCUTOR

Corporal? Corporal Coat? Mister Tambo? Mister Drum! Anybody!

GHOST

There's no one here to come to your aid.

INTERLOCUTOR

Stop! Stop, I know. It is I, I, Corporal Red Coat of the Mounted Police—

GHOST

—Aye, aye!—

INTERLOCUTOR

—cleverly disguised as Sweet Sioux in order to tempt the evil Chief Magistrate to show his true colours.

GHOST

Blast you, Corporal Red Coat. Talk about an Indian giver. Your feminine innocence, your eyes, had me completely convinced.

INTERLOCUTOR

It is now my duty to arrest you, Chief Magistrate.

GHOST

Corporal Coat, could I make you an offer?

INTERLOCUTOR

Oh more villainy. You're trying to bribe me.

GHOST

I offer you the deed to the farm for a taste of your feminine charms.

INTERLOCUTOR

How dare you, sir! Bang bang!

GHOST

Oh I am wounded, I am dying, mortifying, I am dead.

INTERLOCUTOR

Oh Corporal Coat.

GHOST

As my soul slips toward hell, I repent. Is it too late?

INTERLOCUTOR

Call me Red, miss.

GHOST   What a sorry end this is!

INTERLOCUTOR
        I want to thank you.

GHOST   Jesus loves me!

INTERLOCUTOR
        We can talk about that later on, Sioux.

GHOST   And suddenly my skin is white.

INTERLOCUTOR
        Oh, Red, may I offer you some apple cider?

GHOST   Oh miracle! I'm heaven-sent!

INTERLOCUTOR
        I love you.

GHOST   Or are those wedding bells I hear?

INTERLOCUTOR
        I love you, too, my dear. I'm beside myself with love.

GHOST   And as I say adieu to those two united souls, choirs of angels
        remind me how true it is said that the only good Indians are
        the ones who are sainted.

INTERLOCUTOR
        Bravo, Mister Ghost. What a wonderful halo.

GHOST   It's old paint, Mister Interlocutor. Bravo to you, too, sir. I love
        your Sweet Sioux.

INTERLOCUTOR
        As you were. Thank you, thank you, ladies and gentlemen.
        You're too kind.

GHOST   They're deaf, dumb, and blinded by the light of the heavenly
        Ghost, sir.

INTERLOCUTOR
        We hope our tale encouraged all and offended none.

GHOST   There ain't no nuns I can see out there, sir.

INTERLOCUTOR

We give you laughter and tears. We give hope to all who toil and are laden.

GHOST   For every girl, there is a guy.

INTERLOCUTOR

For every man, a maiden.

GHOST   For every nun, a holy Ghost.

SCENE SEVEN

The GHOST, on his way to the footlights, bumps into the placard stand and "Scene Seven: Duet" turns up.

GHOST   Hi, my name's Almighty. Do you come here much?

INTERLOCUTOR

Mister Ghost, where are you going?

GHOST   I want to get in touch with the audience.

INTERLOCUTOR

Our final curtain has yet to descend, Mister Ghost.

GHOST   Speak for yourself. I want to make some new friends in the pit.

INTERLOCUTOR

You can't leave me too.

GHOST   Hiya. Will you help me down?

INTERLOCUTOR

Mister Ghost, I implore you.

GHOST   Mister Interlocutor, sir, or madam, I was forgetting about you.

INTERLOCUTOR

You can't go. I mean, we do have some few ensuing numbers, Mister Ghost.

GHOST   The two of us? Go on without me.

INTERLOCUTOR

None of the rest of our happy company has come along.

GHOST   Look me in the eyes and ask.

INTERLOCUTOR

Please, Mister Ghost. Please.

GHOST   Mister Interlocutor, sir, how do you feel?

INTERLOCUTOR

How do I feel? With my hands! No, Mister Ghost, I feel this
evening like the moon.

GHOST   You feel like the moon, Mister Interlocutor. How is that?

INTERLOCUTOR

Envious and pale of face and alone, Mister Ghost.

GHOST   I know how you feel, but you are mistaken.

INTERLOCUTOR

How am I mistaken, Mister Ghost?

GHOST   The Moon's an old woman. We call her Grandmother. *(to the
tune of "God Save The Queen")*

The Moon's an old woman
A very wise woman.
She's made of light!

GHOST & INTERLOCUTOR

She watches over us,
Over the children
Each of us is a child again
In the coldest night.

INTERLOCUTOR

The Moon's a young woman
A very new woman
Made out of dark
She's waiting for the light
Just as a child might
Wrapped warmly in a blanket and
Not at all afraid.

GHOST   Well how do you feel now, Mister Interlocutor? Mister?

54

SCENE EIGHT

The INTERLOCUTOR, fleeing the GHOST, bumps into the placard stand. "Scene Eight: Stand-up" turns up.

GHOST   Sir!

INTERLOCUTOR
Did you know, Mister Ghost, that marriage is an institution?

GHOST   Yes, sir, I had heard that said.

INTERLOCUTOR
Well, sir, so is an insane asylum! Did you know, Mister Ghost, that love makes the world go round? Well, sir, so does a sock in the jaw! Which reminds me, sir. An Indian from Batoche came up to me the other day and said he hadn't had a bite in days. So I bit him! Do you know, sir, how many Indians it takes to screw in a light bulb?

GHOST   What's a light bulb?

INTERLOCUTOR
Good one, Mister Ghost, a very good one. Well then, sir, if it's nighttime here, it must be winter in Regina. Nothing could be finah than Regina in the wintah, sir. Am I making myself clear? Does this bear repeating? Does this buffalo repeating? Almighty Gas, you say! Answer me, Mister Ghost. Answer! What! A fine time to demand a medium! It's very small of you, sir. I promise you I will large this in your face if you do not choose to co-operate. Tell me, is it true that the Indian brave will marry his wife's sister so he doesn't have to break in a new mother-in-law? Does it therefore follow, sir, that our good and great Queen Victoria keeps her Prince Albert in a can? That's where she keeps the Indians! Hear ye, hear ye! Don't knock off her bonnet and stick her in her royal rump with a sword, sir. The word, sir, is treason. Or are you drunk? Besotted! Be seated, sir. No! Stand up! You, sir, you, I recognize you now. You're that redskin! You're that wagon burner! That feather head, Chief Bullshit. No, Chief

Shitting Bull! Oh, no, no. Bloodthirsty savage. Yes, you're primitive, uncivilized, a cantankerous cannibal! Unruly redman, you lack human intelligence! Stupidly stoic, sick, demented, foaming at the maws! Weirdly mad and dangerous, alcoholic, diseased, dirty, filthy, stinking, ill-fated degenerate race, vanishing, dying, lazy, mortifying, fierce, fierce and crazy, crazy, shit, shit, shit, shit…

GHOST What's a light bulb?

INTERLOCUTOR
Who are you? Who the hell are you?

GHOST I'm a dead Indian. I eat crow instead of buffalo.

IINTERLOCUTOR
That's good. That's very good.

SCENE NINE

The lights shift from variety to spectral as the spotlight finds the placard: "Scene Nine: Finale."

INTERLOCUTOR
Who am I? Do you know?

GHOST I recognized you by your eyes.

INTERLOCUTOR
Who am I?

GHOST White Girl, my White Girl.

INTERLOCUTOR
Who? Who is that?

GHOST My fierce, crazy little girl. My wife. *Ni-wikimakan. [My wife.]*

The INTERLOCUTOR touches her face with her gloved hands as the GHOST embraces and releases her. The spotlight finds her face as her gloved hands begin to wipe the whiteface off, unmasking the woman inside. The GHOST removes one

56

glove and throws it on the dead fire, she does the same with the other. The fire rekindles.

Piko ta-ta-wi kisisomoyan ekwo. [I have to go finish dancing now.]

INTERLOCUTOR

Patima, Kisse-Manitou-Wayou. [Goodbye, Almighty Voice.]

The GHOST goes and dances in celebration to a drum. The woman removes the rest of the whiteface and costume, becoming WHITE GIRL again. She gathers the costume in her arms as the spotlight drifts away to become a full moon in the night. WHITE GIRL lifts a baby-sized bundle to the audience as the GHOST continues to dance in the fading lights.

The end.

ACKNOWLEDGEMENTS

The author thanks the Canada Council for the Arts, Native Earth
Performing Arts, Playwrights' Workshop Montréal, and especially the Banff
Playwrights Colony for help in the development of this play. He is grateful
to Jonathon Fisher, Jani Lauzon, Pamela Mathews, Billy Merasty, Lib Spry,
and especially to Marrie Mumford for their contributions to the process.
Thanks also are due to Floyd Favel and to the doctors Verna J. Kirkness,
UBC, and Ahab Spence, SIFC, for correcting our Cree.

Daniel David Moses is "a coroner of the theatre who slices open the human heart to reveal the fear, hatred and love that have eaten away at it. His dark play... can leave its audience shaking with emotion." (Kate Taylor, *The Globe & Mail*, about *The Indian Medicine Shows*). Moses, a Delaware from the Six Nations lands on the Grand River, lives in Toronto, where he writes, and in Kingston, where he teaches in the Department of Drama at Queen's University.

google scholar

↳ trust —> *JSTOR- *Project Mose